The JFK Assassination

By
Harold Torrance

Cover Graphics by
Jeff Van Kanegan

Inside Illustrations by
Don O'Connor

Cover Photo
The Dallas Morning News

Published by Instructional Fair • TS Denison
an imprint of

About the Author

Harold Torrance has more than ten years experience in teaching, both in middle school and at the elementary level. His areas of specialization include social studies, language arts, and mathematics.

Torrance has had a number of articles published in professional educational journals in the area of mathematics instruction and is also the author of several titles published by Instructional Fair.

Credits

Author: Harold Torrance
Inside Illustrations: Don O'Connor
Photos courtesy of the John Fitzgerald Kennedy Library
Cover Design: Jeff Van Kanegan
Project Director/Editor: Jerry Aten
Editor: Sharon Thompson
Graphic Layout: Jeff Van Kanegan and Sharon Thompson

McGraw-Hill
Children's Publishing

A Division of The McGraw-Hill Companies

Published by Instructional Fair • TS Denison
An imprint of McGraw-Hill Children's Publishing
Copyright © 2002 McGraw-Hill Children's Publishing

Limited Reproduction Permission: Permission to duplicate these materials is limited to the person for whom they are purchased. Reproduction for an entire school or school district is unlawful and strictly prohibited.

Send all inquiries to:
McGraw-Hill Children's Publishing
3195 Wilson Drive NW
Grand Rapids, Michigan 49544

All Rights Reserved • Printed in the United States of America

The JFK Assassination
ISBN: 0-7424-0253-3

3 4 5 6 7 8 9 07 06 05 04 03

Table of Contents

Introduction 4

John Fitzgerald Kennedy 5

    For Further Research 7

Oswald 8

    Questions to Consider 15

Kennedy in Dallas 16

    Questions to Consider 16

The Assassination 17

    Questions to Consider 21

Apprehended! 22

    Questions to Consider 23

Ruby 24

    Questions to Consider 25

The Funeral 26

    Questions to Consider 28

Theories and Discrepancies 29

    Questions to Consider 31

Answers 32

Introduction

The assassination of President John F. Kennedy remains one of the most tragic, shocking, and sad events in all of American history. Virtually every American who was alive on November 22, 1963, remembers where he or she was when hearing the news that the president had been shot. We all have those moments in our lives when events happen that become permanently etched in our minds. The assassination of President Kennedy was one of those events.

Americans took this dreadful act quite personally. It was much more than a crime of one man against another or against a wife and children. It was even more than a blow to humanity. It was considered an assault on the entire American system and struck at the Constitution, the very heart and soul of America.

In the hours and days following President Kennedy's death, other dramatic events unfolded that left the American people and the rest of the world aghast and in search of an explanation for how it all could possibly happen.

Further uncertainty surfaced as Dallas nightclub owner Jack Ruby shot and killed Lee Harvey Oswald, the disgruntled drifter who was charged with President Kennedy's assassination. With Oswald's death came speculation about a possible conspiracy that included many others. Thousands of hours of investigation, volumes of testimony, and many published books and theories later, there remains an air of uncertainty in the minds of many Americans about what really happened. Since that tragic day in Dallas, Americans have been polled at various times and occasions about their opinions on a conspiracy theory. Four decades later many of those polls still indicate that Americans think that JFK's death was more than the action of a lone individual.

The pages that follow were created to give students a substantial coverage of the event beyond that found in typical history textbooks. Firsthand historical accounts, text, and supportive activities will help middle and secondary students to develop a greater appreciation and understanding of this most dramatic and tragic event.

John Fitzgerald Kennedy

President Kennedy and his wife, Jackie, portrayed to the American public an image of success, high energy, and wealth. The couple also presented themselves as an attractive couple, which led the media to refer to their marriage as the perfection found in the mythical Camelot.

Called Jack by his family, John Fitzgerald Kennedy was born on May 29, 1917, in Brookline, Massachusetts. The Kennedy family had first come to the United States in the mid-1800s, its roots stretching back to Ireland. Kennedy's father, Joseph, was a prosperous New England businessman. Young Jack Kennedy enjoyed growing up in a large, wealthy family that stressed both education and hard work as the pillars of success.

John F. Kennedy graduated from Harvard in 1940, practically on the eve of World War II. In 1941 Kennedy entered the Navy and eventually became the skipper of a patrol torpedo boat. In 1943 Kennedy severely injured his back while fighting the Japanese in the Pacific theatre. This injury bothered Kennedy the rest of his life, even impairing him physically at times.

In 1946 Kennedy began his political career, easily being elected to the U.S. Congress from the state of Massachusetts. After three terms in the House, Kennedy beat Henry Cabot Lodge, a member of another old New England family, to win one of Massachusetts' senatorial seats.

During his time in Washington, Kennedy met Jacqueline Lee Bouvier at a dinner party. The two were married in 1953. Jacqueline was intelligent, well spoken, and elegant, making her the ideal wife for a man in politics.

While convalescing from back surgery in 1954, Kennedy wrote *Profiles in Courage*. It was the story of several senators who had taken part in World War II. The book won Kennedy a Pulitzer Prize, well attesting to his writing ability.

By the late 1950s John F. Kennedy began to emerge not only as a U.S. senator from Massachusetts, but as a national figure. He was a man on the rise in his own political party as well. In 1960 Kennedy became the Democratic nominee for president. Kennedy was not only a charismatic personality, but he revealed an incredibly astute political wit by bringing in a powerful southern senator,

Lyndon B. Johnson, as his running mate. This choice effectively sealed a rift that was developing in the party between southern conservatives and more progressively aligned Democrats in the Northeast.

Senator John F. Kennedy met then-Vice President Richard M. Nixon head-on in a series of four televised debates in the closing months of the 1960 presidential campaign. In the first debate, Kennedy outlined and defended positions addressing solutions for hunger in America, the implementation of a minimum wage, health care for the elderly, educational improvements, and the harmful effects of tight money policies. Kennedy posed the question in his opening statement "Are we doing as much as we can do?"

Nixon chose a more pragmatic and less goal-oriented approach in the debates, designed to appeal to a different constituency. The war on Communism, the need for fiscal and budgetary restraint, and his own experience were Nixon's key issues.

By the fourth and final televised debate, many Americans had developed the view of Kennedy as self-assured, a man of ideas and convictions. On the other hand, Nixon had appeared nervous, even sweaty, at times during the debates. His views were seen by many as being simply a promise to extend the uneventful Eisenhower years.

The Nixon-Kennedy debates are still studied by historians and political analysts. To this day, many politicians are reluctant to meet their challengers on a stage, debating ideas in an unobstructed format. Nixon lost the 1960 presidential election to Kennedy by a narrow margin, probably due in part to his lackluster performance in the debates.

As president, Kennedy largely focused his energies on the New Frontier, an ambitious program designed to improve education, uphold civil rights, modernize America's infrastructure, reform the tax code, provide medical care for the elderly, and other broad initiatives addressing the quality of life in America. The Peace Corps was another program promoted by Kennedy. It sent thousands of volunteers abroad to help less-developed nations with agriculture, health care, and schools.

Kennedy is, perhaps, most often faulted for his handling of foreign policy. The Bay of Pigs invasion into Cuba took place only three months after Kennedy became president. Cubans living in the United States, backed by the Central Intelligence Agency, planned an invasion of Cuba in an effort to oust Fidel Castro as Cuba's leader. Kennedy may have been unwilling to prevent a patriotic group of Cubans from retaking their own country from the clutches of a dictator, but he would not commit American forces in the operation. When the invasion failed, Kennedy was blamed for not using America's armed forces. Critics labeled him as being soft on Communism.

In 1962 Kennedy announced a military blockade of Cuba after discovering that Soviet ballistic missiles were being accumulated on the island. Kennedy's softness had been overestimated by the Soviets and now they would see his resolve. The world held its breath for a week, wondering if war would ensue over the Soviets' provocative action. But Kennedy did not blink, and the Soviets chose to retreat rather than test his mettle.

On November 21, 1963, President Kennedy addressed an audience at Brooks Air Force Base in San Antonio, Texas. Many of those in attendance were members of the armed forces, their families, and Texas political figures. Kennedy's speech at this event was a salute to the research being carried out at The Brooks Air Force Base School of Aerospace Medicine and the Aerospace Medical Center.

President Kennedy devoted much of this speech to discussing cutting-edge scientific research being conducted at the base's Aerospace Medical Center. Kennedy stressed the importance of this work and even cited an example of technology being developed that later made the portable heart monitor become a reality.

The speech on this day would be the president's last. He closed this address by relating a story by an Irish writer. In the story a group of boys face a high stone wall that appears to prevent their passing the way they need to go. The boys, determined, toss their hats over the wall, forcing them to find a way to continue. Kennedy closed his speech with this thought, regarding America's Space Program. "This nation has tossed its cap over the wall of space, and we have no choice but to follow it."

For Further Research

Select a topic for further research. Questions have been posed only as clues to guide your research. Write a short paper or prepare an oral presentation to convey your findings.

1. What elements of John F. Kennedy's early background might make one think he would be destined, or even qualified, to become such a leader? In what way was Kennedy's path to the presidency similar to (or different from) that of other presidents?

2. Find out more about the historic Nixon-Kennedy debates of 1960. Do they bear any resemblance to other great historical debates? It has been said that the presidential race in 1960 was "Nixon's to lose." What do you think is meant by that remark? What advantage does a candidate who is behind in the polling have to gain from a debate? What advantage is it for relatively unknown, or third-party, candidates to be included in a political debate?

3. Find out more about U.S.-Cuban relations in the late 1950s and early 1960s. Who was Fidel Castro, and how did he come to power in Cuba? Do you think Kennedy was right to allow the Bay of Pigs invasion to proceed? Should he have committed U.S. forces to such an operation? Do the lessons learned in this situation teach us anything about similar situations that might occur in the future?

4. Kennedy narrowly averted war with the Soviet Union by showing firm resolve during the Cuban Missile Crisis. Do you think U.S. presidents always show a consistent and firm approach when dealing with other countries? In a historical sense, what has been the result at times in the past when the United States has not made its intentions clear? Does the policy matter more than the person in the White House, or are the two the same thing?

Oswald

The name Lee Harvey Oswald was virtually unknown to Americans before the twenty-second day of November 1963. To those who knew him personally, Oswald was regarded as little more than a small-time loser, a young man acutely disenchanted with both America and the American way of life. Had it not been for an extraordinary event, brought about by an almost freakish chain of circumstances, Lee Harvey Oswald would surely have passed into historical obscurity. Today, of course, Oswald is remembered as the assassin of President John Fitzgerald Kennedy. The assassination ensured Oswald's lasting place in history, and far more importantly, changed the probable course of history itself. Would President Kennedy have kept the United States out of a protracted war in Vietnam? What accomplishments would the Kennedy administration have given the world in the months and years beyond November 1963? These questions, forever without answer, have nagged at the collective consciousness of Americans for decades, making JFK's tragic loss even more disturbing.

Understanding Lee Harvey Oswald is, perhaps, the first step in making sense of an otherwise senseless event. Oswald's background, even from early childhood, was characterized by turmoil. His father, Robert, died shortly before Lee Harvey was born on October 18, 1939. His mother, Marguerite, was unable to provide a stable home environment for Lee Harvey and his two brothers. The family moved frequently, and the children spent time in an orphanage when Marguerite was unable to care for them. In 1945 Marguerite married a Dallas businessman, but the relationship was rocky and the marriage did not last. Marguerite's strange behavior in raising young Lee Harvey and his brothers may be explained, in part, by depression or another untreated mental condition. The result was a terrible home life for young Lee Harvey Oswald and his brothers.

Later, teachers, neighborhood kids, and others who had known the young Lee Harvey Oswald would characterize him as an angry loner, subject to unpredictable behavior. In 1948 a shocked neighbor watched as Lee Harvey determinedly chased his older brother, John, through the house with a butcher knife. Marguerite played down the incident as being just a "little scuffle." During a 1952 visit to his brother John in New York, Lee Harvey again brandished a knife and this time used it to threaten his sister-in-law. A pattern of early, violent behavior was emerging in young Oswald.

While in New York, Lee Harvey Oswald attracted the attention of youth authorities there and was ordered by a family court judge to receive care at a home for disturbed boys. With Lee Harvey facing psychiatric evaluation, and possible adjudication to a juvenile facility, Marguerite fled back to New Orleans with her son.

An excerpt from the court report regarding young Lee Harvey Oswald paints a grim picture for his future . . .

> In the case of the minor Lee Harvey Oswald . . . The court-appointed social worker, in conjunction with state-licensed psychiatrists, has found sufficient evidence to indicate Lee needs further examination. Recent family events indicate a pattern of behavior sufficient to indicate the subject's family environment is currently unable to meet this youth's supervision and guardianship needs. Lee is further considered to be truant from school, based on a report submitted by the assistant principal at Lee's last school of record. Subject has missed over 60 percent of school days during the past grading period, indicating once again a pattern . . .

In 1954 Oswald devised a plan to steal guns from a local sporting goods store with the help of a high school classmate. The plan was abandoned when his would-be accomplice insisted that the plan would not work, due to an alarm system installed in the store's window display. What plans did Oswald have for using the guns if the two had been able to steal them? Would the guns have given Oswald the sense of power he lacked? By this time Oswald was already very unhappy with his own life circumstances, but his true motivation for stealing the guns still cannot be explained today with any certainty.

At about this time, Lee Harvey Oswald began reading about Communism. Oswald's fascination with Communism would increase as time passed, eventually becoming fervent support for the political system so unlike that of the United States. In 1956 Oswald wrote the Socialist Party of America to inquire about membership in their youth league. Perhaps Oswald saw in Communism some sense of fairness or opportunity that he felt was lacking in his own experience in America.

Oswald carried his strong views about Communism with him when he enlisted in the Marine Corps in 1956. Joining the Marines would seem a completely contrary action for someone who so admired Marxist-Leninist forms of government. But Oswald's other older brother, Robert, had already served in the Marines. For the younger Lee Harvey, joining the Marines was a way of not only escaping his mother, but also following in his brother's footsteps.

By all accounts Lee Harvey Oswald made a poor Marine. Oswald had taken his outspoken views about Communism with him to the Marines. As a result, he did not get along well with his fellow Marines. Many who knew him also suspected that Oswald was a homosexual, another reason for his not fitting in. However, Oswald did show aptitude in one area during his Marine Corps training. He quickly earned the designation of sharpshooter during basic training. In spite of his adjustment problems in the Marines, Lee Harvey Oswald had proven beyond any doubt that he could use a rifle with expertise.

Oswald was discharged by the Marine Corps in September 1959, his short stint characterized by both disciplinary problems and an inability to get along with peers. Interestingly, Oswald was initially granted an honorable discharge in spite of his poor service record while in the Marines. Almost a year later the oversight was clarified when the Marines amended his discharge to read "undesirable." This action came after a review of Oswald's service records and after considering public statements made by Oswald.

While in the Marines, Oswald had been able to set aside modest savings. Once discharged, he used part of this money to arrange passage on a ship bound for Europe. However, Oswald's intention was not to tour Europe. The Soviet Union was his ultimate destination. Oswald believed that Soviet Russia was a place of equality and opportunity beyond that offered in the United States. He obtained his tourist visa from the Soviet Consulate in Helsinki on October 14, 1959, and arrived in Moscow on October 16.

Lee Harvey Oswald had been in Russia for only two days when he announced to his Russian tourist guide, a KGB informant, that he wished to defect. The Soviets regarded Oswald as a person with little to offer, and they initially refused his request for citizenship. Oswald persisted and was eventually granted permission to stay. He was sent to Minsk, an industrial city, and given a low-level factory job.

By February 1961 Lee Harvey Oswald had lived enough of the Soviet ideal. He wrote the U.S. embassy in Moscow asking to return to the United States. In October 1959 Oswald had renounced his U.S. citizenship and had also left his passport with the American Consul in Moscow. The U.S. State Department was prepared to give Oswald his passport back. It seemed that high-ranking officials in both governments had come to view Lee Harvey Oswald as more bother than he was worth, an impulsive, foolish young man. However, Oswald returned to the United States on June 13, 1962. With him was his Russian-born wife, Marina.

The Oswalds moved to Texas, staying temporarily with Lee Harvey's brother Robert. Lee Harvey Oswald would work a variety of low-paying jobs over the course of the next year. Employers generally found Oswald's job performance unsatisfactory. His pattern of not getting along with others continued. Lee Harvey and Marina also moved in and out of a number of low-rent apartments and rooming houses as Oswald's work situations changed.

Oswald had by now attracted the attention of the Federal Bureau of Investigation. It was not uncommon for the FBI to take an interest in defectors, and in this regard Oswald was no exception. A file was opened on Lee Harvey Oswald, and he was interviewed by FBI agents twice in the latter months of 1962, but no further action was taken regarding his case at that point. Other than Oswald's outspoken views on Communism and his unlikable personal demeanor, agents found no reason to continue monitoring him.

In January 1963 Oswald ordered a .38 caliber Smith & Wesson revolver from a mail-order house in Los Angeles. He used an alias to order the gun, signing A. J. Hidell on the order form. In March, Oswald ordered a 6.5 mm Mannlicher-Carcano rifle from a Chicago-based sporting goods company, also using his Hidell alias. (This rifle was the weapon Oswald would later use to kill President Kennedy. He also used the revolver to kill a Dallas police officer shortly after the Kennedy assassination.)

On Sunday, March 31, 1963, Lee Harvey Oswald posed for a picture in his small backyard. The picture, taken by Marina Oswald, shows Lee Harvey clutching a couple of Communist newspapers in one hand, the Mannlicher-Carcano rifle propped up on his hip. The revolver's handle is prominently shown sticking from his waistband, much in the way of an Old West gunfighter. The picture would later become famous, used by magazines and newspapers over the years as a gruesome trademark of sorts for the disturbed young man.

At about this time, Oswald was plotting the assassination of retired U.S. Army General Edwin Walker. Walker was a political activist, well known in the Dallas area for his ultra-conservative, right-wing views. Interestingly, Walker had been fired from his high-profile job as commander of the 24th Army Division in 1961 by President Kennedy, his outspoken politics shunned even in the somewhat conservative army culture.

Allegedly Oswald tried to kill Walker on the evening of April 10, 1963, as the general sat at his desk working on papers. From the darkness outside Walker's house, Oswald sighted Walker through a window and fired the Mannlicher-Carcano rifle once. The general narrowly escaped death, the bullet deflected by a wooden portion of the window.

About a week after the failed assassination attempt, Lee Harvey Oswald began talking with Marina about moving to New Orleans. Perhaps Oswald was looking for a fresh start, but more likely he wanted out of the Dallas area. Unknown to Oswald, the FBI had reopened his case, having learned more

about Oswald's pro-Communist activities. Oswald arrived in New Orleans in late April and by early May had found a job as a maintenance man at a local coffee company. With the stability of a job, Oswald again concentrated on his political interests. He wrote the national office of the Fair Play for Cuba Committee, a pro-Castro organization, and requested membership. In the same letter, Oswald offered to establish and promote a New Orleans chapter for the group.

By the time Lee Harvey Oswald heard back from the national office of the Fair Play for Cuba Committee, he had already been busy passing out leaflets in the streets of New Orleans, promoting the group. Oswald received his membership card with enthusiasm, and a three-page letter also gave him encouragement about beginning a New Orleans chapter for the group. But as the muggy New Orleans summer of 1963 wore on, Oswald had no success attracting members for the Fair Play for Cuba Committee. He did manage a bit of television publicity for his fledgling New Orleans chapter after a street-corner scuffle with anti-Castro Cubans.

The public scuffle also landed Lee Harvey Oswald in jail overnight. Curiously, Oswald asked to speak to an FBI agent after being interviewed by the New Orleans police. An agent was dispatched to see him and a private interview was held with Oswald at that time. Again in November 1963, only days before the assassination of President Kennedy, Lee Harvey Oswald would initiate contact with the FBI. This time, Oswald personally delivered a sealed envelope addressed to agent James Hosty at the FBI's Dallas office. Unfortunately, the contents of this message will never be known with absolute certainty. Hosty maintained that the note was a warning for him to cease his investigation of Marina Oswald. Hosty also claimed that he destroyed the message at the direction of his immediate superior, J. Gordon Shanklin. Shanklin, however, would later deny Hosty's assertion that the note was destroyed on his orders. Another discovery has made these contacts seem even more compelling: Agent Hosty's name and address information were later found in Lee Harvey Oswald's own address book. In the years after the Kennedy assassination, these contacts with the FBI would become the subject of intense speculation. Numerous theories attempting to explain these events have become cornerstones in the foundation of a subculture which fervently believes that President Kennedy was the victim of a vast murder conspiracy. The FBI's apparent failure to recognize Oswald as a serious threat and its inability to preserve important evidence most likely reflect incompetence on the part of agents directly involved with the case. But based on what is now known, the existing evidence does not point to an agency-wide conspiracy or even a conspiracy among just a few agents.

On September 25, 1963, Lee Harvey Oswald left New Orleans on a bus trip to Mexico City. He had already sent Marina back to Dallas to live temporarily with friends. Oswald's trip to Mexico City represents yet another bizarre turn in his life story. While in Mexico City he met with officials at both the Cuban Embassy and at the Soviet Embassy. It is thought that Oswald was trying to secure permission to travel to Cuba, where he hoped to receive some special recognition or status for the work he had done in New Orleans on behalf of the Cuban cause. Oswald was initially received by officials at both embassies, but it soon became apparent that they were dealing with an unstable person. Oswald was turned away without the travel visas he sought. Once again, Lee Harvey Oswald's grandiose notions of political intrigue had met with failure. A shunned, disappointed Oswald arrived in Dallas on October 3, 1963.

Back in Dallas again, Lee Harvey Oswald began living in cheap rooming houses while he looked for work. Marina continued to stay with friends. Oswald initially had little success finding work, since past employers were not willing to provide good references. It would be a friend of Marina's who finally tracked down a job for Oswald by calling the Texas School Book Depository. The Depository served as a warehouse and distribution facility for school textbooks, and at the time the Depository was in need of temporary employees. During a short interview with the warehouse supervisor, Oswald told numerous lies about his background. As a result of the interview, Lee Harvey Oswald received a job offer and began work at the Texas School Book Depository on October 16, 1963. In just a little over a month from that time, Oswald would conceal himself in a corner of the sixth floor of the Depository building and use the unobstructed view it afforded to fire his Mannlicher-Carcano rifle at the slow-moving presidential motorcade.

Lee Harvey Oswald gradually settled into something of a routine working as a loading clerk at the Depository. Unlike other jobs he had held, he managed to perform this job well enough to keep it. Unknown to Oswald at the time, the FBI had again opened his file as a result of his unusual trip to Mexico City. By early November, Oswald became aware of the FBI monitoring his activities. Days ticked by without the impulsive Oswald tipping his hand.

On November 16 the *Dallas Times Herald* published the route that would be used by President Kennedy's motorcade in the upcoming trip to Dallas. Oswald probably learned of the route by reading newspapers that were routinely left in the employee break room. Oswald would have studied the newspaper accounts of President Kennedy's upcoming visit, just as he had previously studied General Edwin Walker's routines. This time, the events set into motion would have a tragic conclusion for the nation. At age 24 Lee Harvey Oswald, a complete failure at nearly everything he had ever tried, would have his one brief moment of "success" on November 22, 1963.

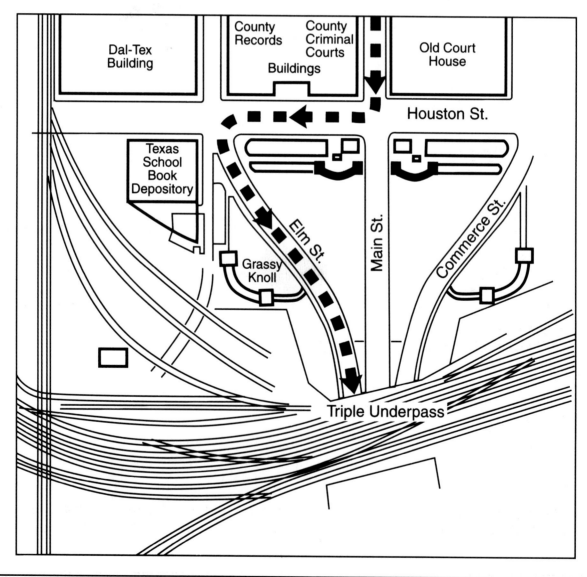

A True Eyewitness Account: The amazing case of Yuri Nosenko. In January 1964 a highly placed Soviet intelligence officer would approach CIA agents at a secret meeting in Geneva, Switzerland. Colonel Yuri Nosenko, a KGB officer, brought with him a wealth of secrets about Soviet Russia when he defected to the United States. It had only been a scant two months since President Kennedy's assassination, and the CIA was now presented with a man knowledgeable about Lee Harvey Oswald's period of time in Russia.

The CIA, initially suspicious of Nosenko, imprisoned him in a secret facility outside Washington, D.C. It was not until 1968 that a new CIA director began to question Nosenko's detention and the failure of underlings to exploit what the valuable defector knew. Agency personnel came to view Nosenko in a different light when information he provided turned out to be true, leading to the capture of a number of Soviet spies in Europe. Nosenko's information in a variety of matters turned out to be reliable, and therefore very valuable.

Nosenko maintained Oswald's defection had not been encouraged by the Soviets. On the contrary, after interviewing him, the KGB found Oswald to be of no practical use, even considering him a liability. Oswald was only allowed to remain in Russia after he had attempted to kill himself in his hotel room. Soviet officials decided to let Oswald stay only after weighing the possible international implications if Oswald killed himself while still in Russian custody. Even Soviet Russia had not wanted anything to do with the disturbed young man, Lee Harvey Oswald.

Questions to Consider

1. How might Lee Harvey Oswald's life have been different had he grown up in a more stable environment?

2. Why do you think Oswald was ultimately unable to live and work in Soviet Russia?

3. How did Oswald's strong attitudes and beliefs affect his ability to be successful in an ordinary job setting?

4. Why do you think Oswald was so eager to be accepted by a group such as the Fair Play for Cuba Committee?

5. How is Oswald's trip to Mexico City in 1963 similar to his previous defection to the Soviet Union?

6. Although it is unclear exactly when Oswald learned of the route to be used by the presidential motorcade, do you think he put much thought into his decision to kill President Kennedy?

7. How might the defection of KGB officer Yuri Nosenko have aided the investigation of the Kennedy Assassination?

Kennedy in Dallas

John F. Kennedy had gone to Texas in November 1963 for a reason. Politics drove the visit. There was a presidential election only a scant year away, and Texas was an important state in deciding the contest. This trip to Texas would be a preliminary run, looking to shore up support there. Even Jacqueline Kennedy, the elegant first lady, was along, not only as company for JFK, but also for the political advantage to be gained from her presence.

Vice President Lyndon Johnson was also along on this trip, a Texan back in his home state to crunch out promises of support from the numerous political cronies he would be meeting with on this trip. Johnson was known as a political mover, a shrewd player who could make things happen by drawing on his contacts and pressing them for results. Texas Governor John Connally would join the two men in this political operation, his own stature being enhanced by the limousine ride he would share with the president as the men rode through Dallas together.

As a city, Dallas had something of a right-wing reputation. The town and most of its population were considered to be conservative. Even the Democrats there were conservative. Although Kennedy was himself a Democrat, he represented a kind of progressive New England-style Democrat quite different from those in the South. Many in his own party, particularly in the South, resented Kennedy's views. Some felt that there had been too much said about civil rights and not enough done about Communist Cuba. This was the political climate faced by President Kennedy on his trip to Dallas in November 1963.

Robert MacNeil, who was covering President Kennedy's trip to Dallas for NBC News, made this comment:

> "It was significant that Kennedy had chosen to attack the spirit that had made Dallas such a nest of extremists. Right-wing demonstrators had assaulted fellow Texan Lyndon Johnson during the 1960 campaign. Just a few weeks before the Kennedy visit, U.N. Ambassador Adlai Stevenson had been spat upon and struck with posters. Dallas officials were determined there would be no repetition of such incidents; Dallas police had mounted the biggest security operation in the city's history. That was the atmosphere that awaited Kennedy, and in which he would deliver his provocative remarks."

Questions to Consider

1. Why is Texas considered such an important state in presidential elections?

2. Why do presidents often have such a difficult time consolidating support, even within their own political party?

3. Given the political climate of the city, why do you think Kennedy chose Dallas for his visit instead of another Texas city?

The Assassination

On the morning of November 22, 1963, Lee Harvey Oswald broke from his normal routine. He had been in the habit of waiting for an acquaintance from work to pick him up, but on this particular morning he walked the short distance to meet his ride at his home. Oswald's work mate would notice that he was carrying a long package wrapped in brown paper. When asked about the package, Lee Harvey Oswald would tell the acquaintance that it was a bundle of curtain rods. Apparently, the package did not arouse anyone's suspicion. Oswald carried it with him when he entered the Texas School Book Depository that morning.

On the sixth floor of the Depository, workers were installing a new plywood floor. The sixth floor of the Depository was essentially a large, square, open storage room with dimensions of ninety-six feet on each side. On this day the sixth floor would have had books stacked in various spots as the crew moved them around to get at the flooring job. Tools and construction materials scattered about would also have added to the disarray. Lee Harvey Oswald was seen by workers on the sixth floor at approximately 11:40 a.m. Oswald was at the window on the east end of the Depository. These windows overlooked Dealey Plaza and the route that President Kennedy's motorcade would shortly be following. About five minutes later, the flooring crew left for lunch break.

Once alone, Lee Harvey Oswald went to work arranging boxes of books in the southeast corner of the sixth floor. The boxes would conceal him from view if someone happened upstairs during the lunch hour. This corner of the building would have given Oswald a commanding view of the motorcade as it approached Dealey Plaza and as it made the slow turn going down Elm Street. Once secure in his sniper's nest, Oswald would have set about assembling the Mannlicher-Carcano rifle. Oswald waited for the motorcade.

At 12:29 the first car of President Kennedy's motorcade arrived, turning onto Houston Street. It was a security vehicle containing local police and Secret Service Agent Forrest Sorrels. The next vehicle was the presidential limousine. President Kennedy and First Lady Jacqueline were seated in the back. Texas Governor John Connally and his wife were in the front. Their driver was a veteran Secret Service agent who would later be criticized for his sluggish reaction when the first shot was fired. The next vehicle carried only Secret Service agents and presidential aides. Other vehicles carrying Vice-President Johnson, local officials, and members of the press followed.

By this point, Lee Harvey Oswald would have been studying the motorcade's approach with the practiced eye of a sharpshooter assessing his target. Within seconds he would have positioned his rifle across the box of books he had previously arranged as a rifle rest. Secret Service Agent Forrest Sorrels would look at his watch at almost 12:30 as the presidential limousine

slowed to turn onto Elm Street. Throngs of people had come to see the president, and the crowd might have been even larger due to the lunch hour. At about this moment, Mrs. Connally turned and directed this comment to JFK: "Mr. President, you can't say that Dallas doesn't love you!" President Kennedy would respond, "No, you certainly can't." Those would be the president's last words.

Within seconds a shot rang out. Many startled witnesses would later say it sounded like the backfire of a car. A second shot quickly sounded, and President Kennedy appeared to be gripping his throat in a grim reaction to the noise. Doctors would later explain this as being a neurological response to the bullet, which had entered the back of his neck and exited just below his Adam's apple. The same bullet struck Governor Connally, sitting just in front of the president, causing him extensive injury, but not resulting in a fatal wound. At this point Connally shouted, "My God, they are going to kill us all!"

Larry O'Brien, who was JFK's Congressional Liaison at the time of the assassination, gave this account:

"Kennedy's car was four or five cars ahead of us and we could see him waving to the crowds. ... On the outskirts of Dallas, the crowds were large, but not enthusiastic. My impression was that they'd come out of curiosity and perhaps to glimpse Jackie. The mood changed, however, as we entered downtown Dallas. Suddenly there were cheering crowds pressing in on the motorcade and throwing confetti. The scene reminded me of New York City's Broadway ... We were rounding a corner when we heard a shot. What was that? I immediately asked our driver. I don't know, he said. They must be giving him a twenty-one gun salute. As he spoke we heard additional shots. We had no idea what had happened."

Ten-year-old Rosemary Willis was running alongside the presidential motorcade as it proceeded slowly down Elm Street. She is seen clearly in the famous Zapruder film, an 8mm home movie taken by Abraham Zapruder. The film captures the entire assassination event and has over the years been used for studying the assassination. After the first shot Rosemary Willis is seen in the film halting her gleeful chase of the motorcade, and turning to look at the Texas School Book Depository. Later she would explain her behavior by saying she had heard a shot fired and looked to see where it had come from.

President Kennedy, strapped into a back brace, was unable to clear himself from the line of fire. Jacqueline Kennedy leaned toward JFK. She realized that something must be wrong. Even the driver had slowed the car at this point, turning to see what was happening in the back seat. The third and final bullet then struck Kennedy in the right side of his head. While it is speculated that Kennedy might have survived his neck wound had he received treatment, the third shot tore away a portion of his skull. This third shot was Lee Harvey Oswald's killing shot. Three spent cartridges found on the Depository's sixth floor in the sniper's nest would bear grim testimony to this fact.

I was the editor on duty at KMTV in Omaha when the news first came clattering across UPI.

I had to get the story on the air as the network was down at the time to allow for local programming.

I remember thinking this is a new time in our lives.

—Tom Brokaw

John Fitzgerald Kennedy was rushed to Parkland Hospital, where doctors worked feverishly to assess his condition. Attempts to treat the president were ineffective. He had no pulse, and only shallow, spasmodic breathing was observed. The team of doctors treating President Kennedy fixed the time of death at 1:00 p.m. Central Standard Time. Vice-President Lyndon Johnson, waiting in a nearby room at the hospital, was notified shortly thereafter.

Under heavy security, Johnson was rushed from Parkland Hospital and taken to Love Field. The presidential airplane, *Air Force One*, was there waiting at Love Field. From the plane, Johnson would speak with Robert Kennedy, the president's brother and attorney general of the United States. Robert Kennedy was uncertain of the precise legal process to transfer power. Within minutes, an assistant attorney general called back to give Johnson instructions regarding the legal transfer of power. It was decided that the transfer of power should take place without delay.

Shortly after 2:00 p.m., Jacqueline Kennedy arrived at the airport in the ambulance containing President Kennedy's body. There had been some confusion at the hospital with a local official over the movement of the president's body. The Secret Service had expedited the process by appropriating the necessary vehicles, including an ambulance. The coffin containing President John F. Kennedy's body was loaded onto *Air Force One* at 2:18 p.m.

> On that November day, . . . I remember that I climbed down from the seat of a tractor, unhooked a farm trailer, and walked into my warehouse to weigh a load of grain. I was told by a group of farmers that the president had been shot. I went outside, knelt on the steps, and began to pray.
> —Jimmy Carter

The group waited for the arrival of a federal judge, Sarah Hughes, who could officially administer the oath of office to Lyndon Johnson. By 2:47 the country had a new president and *Air Force One* was bound for Washington, D.C.

Jack Valenti, who would later become president of the Motion Picture Association of America, was in the Kennedy motorcade that day and was also a close friend of President Kennedy. He was terribly shaken over the events and was aboard *Air Force One* when it flew back to Washington, D.C., from Dallas with the president's body aboard. Below is Valenti's account of the trip back to Washington, D.C.

In the aft portion of the plane rested the body of John Kennedy, forever enclosed in a flag-draped coffin. I was witness to the swearing in of the new president, his wife and Mrs. Kennedy by his side as he took the oath which resides in the Constitution. I learned then from personal anguish/experience that while the light in the White House may flicker, the light in the White House never goes out. The country goes on. That's what this country is all about."

Questions to Consider

1. In the years since JFK's assassination, the Secret Service has become far more sophisticated in their efforts to protect the president. What measures do you think could have been taken even in 1963 to better ensure President Kennedy's safety?

2. Lyndon Johnson received some criticism for his hasty assumption of power, literally within minutes after Kennedy's death. Do you think the criticism was warranted? Explain your reasons.

Apprehended!

Numerous other witnesses would also hear the shots and, like Rosemary Willis, would turn their attention to the Texas School Book Depository. One of these people was newsman Robert MacNeil.

I really started to believe there was shooting because on the grass on both sides of the roadway people were throwing themselves down and covering their children with their bodies. I saw people running up the grassy hill beside the road. I thought they were chasing whoever had done the shooting and I ran after them. It did not enter my head that Kennedy had been hit. I ran into the first building I came to that looked as though it might have a phone. It was the Texas Book Depository. As I ran up the steps and through the door, a young man in shirt sleeves was coming out. In great agitation I asked him where there was a phone. He pointed inside to an open space where another young man was talking on a phone situated near a pillar and said, 'Better ask him.' I found a phone on the desk.

Oswald left the Depository and began walking east on Elm Street. He spotted a bus near the corner of St. Paul and, rushing to it, pounded at the bus door for entry. The driver would later remember Oswald because of the urgency in which he boarded. Another witness, Oswald's former landlady, would also be able to establish him as being on the bus at that time. When traffic looked to be stalled only a short time later, Oswald got off the bus. Walking a few blocks, he hailed a cab that took him to his rooming house.

At his room, Oswald hurriedly collected his .38 revolver and a jacket. Although it was late November, the weather was quite warm and Oswald probably took the jacket with him to conceal the gun more easily. Oswald quickly left the rooming house without speaking to the housekeeper, who had tried to engage Oswald in conversation as he was leaving.

At about 1:15, Officer J. D. Tippit spotted Oswald walking along Tenth Street, placing Oswald about a mile from his rooming house. Lee Harvey Oswald had left the Depository in a rush, stopped to pick up a pistol at his room, and with very little cash in his pocket, about $14, was trying to put distance between himself and places where he could be found easily. There can be no doubt that Lee Harvey Oswald was in flight at this point, having committed the biggest crime in American history since Abraham Lincoln's murder nearly a hundred years before.

Officer Tippit must have thought that Oswald resembled the description of the president's assassin being broadcast over the police radio. Police all over Dallas were, at that moment, stopping people with routine questions and following up on leads. When Tippit pulled up alongside Oswald and got out of his patrol car, he must have been only curious about Oswald at that point. Tippit had not drawn his revolver as he walked toward the front of the patrol car. Oswald was seen by witnesses as he drew his own pistol and fired, hitting Tippit four times. Officer J. D. Tippit was found dead at the scene when help for him arrived shortly.

Lee Harvey Oswald was next seen by numerous witnesses running through residential yards and across parking lots. Oswald managed to reload his pistol while fleeing from the Tippit murder scene. Entering a business district, Oswald's hurried, suspicious behavior began attracting attention. Oswald ducked into a shoe store briefly, waiting for police cars to pass on the street. From the shoe store Oswald went to the Texas Theater, skirting inside without bothering to pay for a ticket. By now Oswald would have been desperate for a quiet place to avoid capture while he thought about his next move.

Theater employees, suspicious of Oswald and at the same time aware that an assassin was being sought, called the police. Dallas Police apprehended Oswald in the Texas Theater after a short scuffle. During the course of the scuffle, Oswald once again pulled his revolver, intending to use it on another police officer. But this time no shots were fired.

Oswald was taken to the Dallas Police Station, where pieces of the grim puzzle were already being put together by investigators.

Questions to Consider

1. What aspects of Lee Harvey Oswald's behavior after the assassination indicate that he was behaving like a guilty person?

2. If Oswald had not been apprehended at the Texas Theater, do you suppose he might have been able to slip away from police and ultimately elude capture?

3. Historians have drawn several dramatically chilling parallels between the events that surrounded the assassination of President Lincoln with that of President Kennedy. Research the facts behind this comparison between the two assassinations and record your findings to be shared with other members of your class.

Ruby

On the morning of November 24, 1963, Jack Ruby made his way down the ramp leading into the Dallas Police Department's underground parking garage. The police officer guarding the ramp was either distracted by a car leaving the garage, or perhaps he recognized Ruby's face as familiar around the police station. The circumstances surrounding Ruby's entrance to the garage have long been a source of controversy, but Ruby did enter the garage, apparently without being stopped.

Ruby was seen by a television news director at the bottom of the garage ramp only a half-minute or so before Lee Harvey Oswald was to be led through the garage to a waiting police car. Since his apprehension by Dallas Police, Oswald had been at the Dallas Police Station. After extensive interrogations, he was being moved to the Sheriff's Department jail facilities. When Oswald appeared in the custody of a group of policemen, Jack Ruby was there waiting.

As Lee Harvey Oswald was being led past, Jack Ruby lunged forward. Thrusting his .38-caliber revolver at Oswald, Ruby fired a single shot at near point-blank range. Ruby was quickly wrestled to the ground by police. A television crew there to cover the transfer captured the entire event on film. The bullet struck Oswald in the upper abdomen, a perfect killing shot. An ambulance arrived in only minutes, taking Oswald to Parkland Hospital, the same facility where President Kennedy had been declared dead only two days before. But surgeons there could do little for Lee Harvey Oswald. The president's assassin was now dead and would remain forever silent about his role in the assassination.

Jack Leon Ruby began life as Jacob Rubenstein on March 25, 1911, born into a Jewish family in one of Chicago's tougher neighborhoods. (He would not become Jack Leon Ruby until 1947, when he had his name legally changed.) Ruby grew up in a chaotic household similar to that of Lee Harvey Oswald. His mother was unable to control him as a child. Jack Ruby grew up streetwise with a reputation for fighting. Ruby scalped tickets, sold gambling tip sheets, and peddled small merchandise on the streets to earn money.

Jack Ruby moved to Dallas in 1947, where he became a partner with his sister in the nightclub business. In spite of this line of work, it is unlikely that Ruby was working for organized crime or had any substantial business links with organized crime. Ruby owned a string of failed nightclubs in Dallas over the years leading up to the Kennedy assassination, but he never attained the kind of stature from these enterprises that he had hoped for. Jack Ruby was considered small-time, something of an attention seeker, by nearly all who knew him.

Ruby was something of a police groupie. He handed out free passes to policemen for his clubs and further encouraged them by giving out free drinks when they visited the clubs. Ruby fostered these relationships over a period of years and certainly knew dozens of Dallas policemen. Ruby might also have enhanced his stature with the police by acting as an informer. Jack Ruby was also arrested a number of times for assault and other lesser violations but never managed to land in serious trouble. Perhaps Ruby sought police attention as a nightclub owner since he knew that, from time to time, he would need to call on them for favors. For this reason it is unlikely that Ruby would have been trusted by organized crime, due to the close association he sought with the police. A link between Jack Ruby and organized crime, long bandied about by conspiracy buffs, seems an unlikely scenario due to Ruby's ties with the police.

Jack Ruby's whereabouts during the Kennedy assassination appear to have been well documented. A number of witnesses place Ruby at the offices of the *Dallas Morning News* well before the assassination, as early as 11:00 a.m. Ruby had business in the advertising offices there, but it was typical Jack Ruby behavior to seek out other acquaintances and to talk to them as well. As a result, a number of employees were later able to place Jack Ruby there during the time of the assassination. Ruby was actually there to pay for ads for his nightclub and to work with an advertising department employee on the content for those ads. Ruby was apparently still at the offices of the *Dallas Morning News* after word had reached the staff there that President Kennedy had been shot. This would seem to refute theories involving Ruby in a plot to kill Kennedy. Since he was at the newspaper offices, he could not have physically fired a second weapon at President Kennedy.

People who knew Jack Ruby would later characterize him as being quite upset over the assassination. Ruby closed his nightclub, telling people it was out of respect for the president. He did not tell employees exactly when they would reopen, but it was assumed in a few days.

That afternoon a newspaper reporter who knew Jack Ruby observed him at Parkland Hospital. Ruby would later turn up that evening at the Dallas Police Station. Ruby's appearance at these places clearly demonstrated that he liked being near the center of attention. Later, newspaper reporters and policemen also placed him on the third floor, where Lee Harvey Oswald was being interrogated. Ruby would come within just a few feet of Oswald that evening as police led Oswald to a press conference. Ruby even drew further attention to himself that night by being prominently photographed at the press conference with reporters.

Saturday afternoon, Jack Ruby again visited the third floor of the Dallas Police Station. Jack Ruby's true motivation for killing Lee Harvey Oswald will never be known. Certainly, his pending trial must have guided Ruby's willingness to be forthcoming with the entire truth. In 1964 Ruby was convicted of Oswald's murder. Ruby's health, especially his mental condition, deteriorated steadily while he was incarcerated. In 1966 the Texas Court of Criminal Appeals granted Ruby a new trial. But Jack Ruby died on January 3, 1967, before his new trial could begin. He had apparently been suffering from an undiagnosed case of cancer of the lungs, liver, and brain for at least a year prior to his death.

Questions to Consider

1. From what you now know about Jack Ruby, what can be said about his motivation for killing Lee Harvey Oswald?

2. It has been hypothesized that Ruby killed Oswald on impulse, having unexpectedly been presented with the opportunity on November 24, 1963. If you were a prosecutor, how would you make your case that Ruby had planned to commit this murder?

The Funeral

The funeral of President Kennedy on Monday, January 25, 1963, was one of the saddest days in American history. The line waiting to pass by the coffin, which was lying in state on the Lincoln catafalque in the rotunda under the dome in the Capitol, was still three miles long at 6:00 a.m. on the morning of the funeral. Over 250,000 American mourners would file past his casket prior to the funeral.

Congressman (and later U.S. Senator) Charles Mathias from Maryland said of the meeting of the Cabinet and members of Congress in the rotunda,

"We gathered in complete quiet. The eloquent men, the great orators of the Congress, all stood silent with heads bowed and centered in attention and emotion on the casket carrying the body of the 35th president of the United States. As the pallbearers bore the casket from the rotunda, every soul in that assemblage was wretched by the human suffering of Mrs. Kennedy and her children—that suffering, which she subdued because the wife of a president is not even allowed the privilege of her grief, but must uphold the traditions of the office to which her husband had been called."

After Jackie, Robert, and Ted Kennedy kneeled by the casket, the procession left Capitol Hill for the White House and then on to St. Matthew's Cathedral. When the caisson arrived at the White House, the 11 Chiefs of State formed a single line so that no one would be behind another. As a concern for security, Undersecretary George Ball was asked to remain behind at the White House. With all of the foreign heads of state as well as the many American dignitaries and statesmen, there was fear that another assassination attempt might be made during the funeral procession.

President Lyndon Johnson, who was a member of the procession, said, "The muffled rumble of drums set up a heartbreaking echo."

While almost everyone admitted to St. Matthew's Cathedral was either an American or foreign dignitary, Jackie sent passes to the four private citizens who had been crew members of PT-109, which her husband had helped to rescue in August of 1943. Gerald Zilger, one of the men said,

> "There weren't very many of us "regular" people allowed inside."

Cardinal Richard Cushing of Boston, who presided at the funeral, began "May the angels, dear Jack, lead you into paradise. May the martyrs receive you and your coming." As the casket was removed from the cathedral and placed on the caisson, President Kennedy's son, John, Jr., saluted the casket.

Other onlookers made the following observations:

"It was the saddest thing I ever saw. Some of the people were sadder than if a relative had died."

"I could actually hear people sobbing."

"Some people had sort of a frightened look, like what are we going to do now?"

A member of the Marine Band which led the funeral procession on the seven-mile journey to Arlington National Cemetery made this comment:

> "To see Americans standing eight to ten feet deep along a seven-mile route to get a look at a flag-draped caisson go by is the most moving sight I ever experienced in my time with the band."

Black Jack, the riderless horse, pranced nervously, and the man in charge of holding him in check feared for the entire procession that the horse might bolt from his grip. When the cortege reached Arlington, the Marine Band played "The Star-Spangled Banner," the Air Force Bagpipes played, and the coffin was raised from the caisson and carried to the grave. Fifty jet fighters flying in a V formation, with the last plane missing to symbolize the fallen leader, flew over, followed by *Air Force One*, which dipped its wing in honor of the fallen president as it passed over Arlington National Cemetery.

After the 21-gun salute, a lone bugler sounded the doleful notes of taps, and the flag that had been draped over the casket was folded and presented to Mrs. Kennedy. She then lit the Eternal Flame, ending the service, and perhaps the saddest day in modern-day America came to an end. Arthur Schlesinger, who served as Special Assistant to both Presidents Kennedy and Johnson, reflects on the transferring of the flame to the Lincoln Memorial:

> "On December 22, a month after his death, fire from the flame burning at his grave at Arlington was carried at dusk to the Lincoln Memorial. It was fiercely cold. Thousands stood, candles in their hands as the flame spread among us, one candle lighting the next as the crowd gently moved away, the torches flaring and flickering, into darkness. The next day it snowed—almost as deep a snow as the inaugural blizzard. I went to the White House. It was lovely, ghostly strange. It all ended, as it began, in the cold."

Questions to Consider

1. David Bruce reported from London, "Great Britain has never before mourned a foreigner as it has President Kennedy. As the news spread around London, thousands of people came to sign the condolence book." Similar kinds of actions were apparent all over the world. Why do you suppose the death of President Kennedy had such an impact on people from other countries?

2. It has been said that the funeral of President Kennedy forever changed the face of politics in America. The loss of innocence felt by Americans was further intensified by events in the sixties that followed. Research the logic behind these statements and find out why millions of young Americans changed their outlook on life forever.

Theories and Discrepancies

It is the most controversial case in modern American history. Did Lee Harvey Oswald kill President Kennedy by himself, or was it a conspiracy? And if there was a conspiracy, did it include Oswald?

In the very hours after President John F. Kennedy's assassination, numerous theories were spawned in an effort to explain the events surrounding the president's death. As time wore on and questions remained unanswered, conspiracies were fashioned from rumors and fragments of fact, almost in the way a quilt is pieced together by an experienced quilter. Portions were added or taken away, meanings shaded to support a particular point of view, and kernels of truth made to blossom into total works of fiction. Facts were invented, ignored, manipulated, and sometimes concealed. People were thrown (or in many cases voluntarily leaped) into this mix, including government officials, eye witnesses to the events, attention-seekers, book promoters, political activists, people who knew the major players, people who knew of plots, and people who actually knew nothing but pretended to know more. As a result, many otherwise prudent people found themselves believing outlandish scenarios regarding President Kennedy's death. Over the years a number of polls have even indicated that the American public by and large believes that JFK was killed as the result of a conspiracy, as opposed to the actions of a lone individual.

The previous selections in this book were written in an attempt to provide a factual overview of the events surrounding President Kennedy's assassination. Still, lingering questions do remain about the assassination. In an effort to provide a balance, this final section was created to introduce some of those discrepancies, without necessarily endorsing any of them.

The Grassy Knoll—Of all the persistent conspiracy theories, the Grassy Knoll theory has taken on a substantial stature, assuming an almost provable (but just not yet proven) status. It is probably the most widely accepted of all the conspiracy theories. The term *grassy knoll* describes an area bordering Dealey Plaza that is essentially a raised section of ground overlooking Elm Street. In 1963 a large railroad transfer yard was located behind the grassy knoll area.

The Grassy Knoll theory proposes that another assassin, or an organized team of assassins, fired from behind the protection of a wooden fence along the grassy knoll, killing JFK and leaving Oswald as a "patsy" for the crime. Interestingly, some witnesses at Dealey Plaza steadfastly insisted that a shot or shots came from the grassy knoll area. After the motorcade passed, people climbed the grassy knoll and began looking for signs of another shooter. Federal agents considered the area important enough to cordon off and search. There also have been lingering reports over the years of people with either false uniforms or false identification who were present on the knoll, perhaps aiding the escape of assassins or foiling the early investigation.

Worth mentioning is the testimony of Lee Bowers before the Warren Commission. (The

Warren Commission was a special fact-finding commission led by Earl Warren, Chief Justice of the U.S. Supreme Court. Much has been discovered about the assassination in the years since the Warren Commission, which concluded that Oswald acted alone.) Bowers was employed to operate the railroad signal tower in the rail yard behind the grassy knoll. It gave him a second-story view of the grassy knoll area from only 130 feet away. It has been asserted that Bowers would have been busy with his regular duties, perhaps too busy to be a particularly useful witness. But how many people working a mundane job would be more interested in seeing a special once-in-a-lifetime event (such as a presidential motorcade passing by) than concentrating on the sort of work which they did each day?

Bowers mentioned three cars circling the yard's lot in a parking area. The cars left, but did Bowers miss them discharging passengers or leaving behind equipment? Bowers also described a "commotion" in the parking area behind the fence, but "nothing that I could pinpoint as having happened."

Was Lee Bowers telling the truth? Was he telling all he knew about the incidents that day on the grassy knoll? Probably, but Bowers died in a 1966 single-automobile accident when his car ran off the road into a concrete abutment.

The Clay Shaw Trial—Jim Garrison, the flamboyant district attorney of New Orleans, brought charges against prominent New Orleans businessman Clay Shaw in 1967. The primary charge, conspiracy to murder the president of the United States, would draw national attention to the city famous for its Cajun cuisine and Mardi Gras celebrations.

Garrison's case, supported with little hard evidence, rested on proving that Clay Shaw was a kingpin in a far-reaching conspiracy to kill the president. Garrison tried to link Shaw to David Ferrie and Guy Banister. Ferrie was a soldier-of-fortune pilot with possible ties to the CIA. Guy Banister was a former FBI agent who ran a detective agency. Garrison maintained that the three had ties to anti-Communist Cubans, interested in the overthrow of Fidel Castro's government. Oswald's link to this group was never clearly demonstrated, although it was rumored that Oswald had been part of Ferrie's Civil Air Patrol unit when he was 15.

One piece of hard evidence did exist which seemed to tie Oswald to Banister. Some of the leaflets handed out by Oswald containing his Fair Play for Cuba Committee message were stamped 544 Camp St. This address was for the same building from which Guy Banister ran his detective agency. One side of this building did indeed front on 544 Camp Street. Many people cite this as evidence of Oswald's status as some sort of intelligence agent for either a government agency or secret private organization.

Guy Banister died from a heart attack in 1964. Conspiracy theorists cite the number of drugs available to induce heart failure. If this is to be believed, then precisely who wanted Guy Banister dead? David Ferrie died in 1967, practically on the eve of Clay Shaw's trial. If Jim Garrison was getting close to the truth, then David Ferrie's death would have served to silence him in regard to the investigation into Shaw. However, David Ferrie died of a brain aneurysm, unless Ferrie's death was induced by something unnatural.

After an extensive series of legal proceedings, District Attorney Jim Garrison was unable to secure a conviction against Clay Shaw in a court of law. Garrison drew much criticism for his tactics, the unreliable witnesses he relied on, and the often outlandish theories he put forward. Garrison's pursuit of Shaw was finally ruled to be in excess of that reasonably allowed under the law. In 1971 a federal court barred Garrison from taking further legal action against Shaw. Clay Shaw died in 1974 of cancer. However, the conspiracy theory involving Clay Shaw is still alive today.

John Connally—More obscure is the theory that Kennedy might not have been the primary target of Oswald's attack. Oswald's true motivation for killing JFK cannot be determined with total certainty, since Oswald was killed by Jack Ruby only two days later. Interestingly, Oswald had written to John Connally in 1962 regarding his Marine Corps discharge. In his letter, Oswald asked Connally, a former Secretary of the Navy, to assist in upgrading his discharge to honorable. On November 22, 1963, Lee Harvey Oswald might have been trying to settle a score with John Connally for his refusal to help upgrade Oswald's discharge. Was JFK simply in the line of fire when Oswald tried to kill John Connally? The world will never know for certain.

Two Deranged Men Theory—Many Americans felt that Lee Harvey Oswald was an unstable man and was deranged when he assassinated President Kennedy. Many of those same people felt that Jack Ruby was also unstable and perhaps in a fit of outrage at what had happened, he acted alone when he killed Oswald.

The above are just some of the many, many "explanations" and theories that have surfaced, been advanced, explored, and debated on what really happened that horrible day in Dallas. While the findings of the Warren Commission were acceptable to some Americans, many others were left with a dissatisfied empty feeling that the truth lay much deeper than the official published conclusions. Unfortunately, this terrible tragedy will probably always remain as the greatest unsolved mystery in American history.

Questions to Consider

1. If the premise that Lee Harvey Oswald did not act alone is to be accepted, why does the Grassy Knoll theory seem to provide the best fit for that premise?

2. Why do you think District Attorney Jim Garrison pursued Clay Shaw in such an aggressive way? Would his reasons seem to be justified or not?

3. Conspiracies of any variety rely on the parties involved to maintain secrecy, or the conspiracy could be revealed. How likely would it be for a group of people to carry out a crime such as the assassination of JFK and yet have none of the elements of that conspiracy proven after nearly four decades?

4. What type of new evidence would need to be uncovered to substantially change the accepted account of JFK's death? Would it be believable if a person with no physical evidence came forward to accept blame as being part of a conspiracy (to date many have)? How about new papers and documents being discovered? Secret recordings? Previously unknown photographs?

Answers

Oswald
Questions to Consider—page 15
Answers will vary for all questions in this section. Suggestions are provided only for some questions.
2. Oswald was unlikely to be happy anywhere.
3. Oswald was clearly inflexible in his political views and on a personal level not easy to interact with in the workplace.
4. Oswald probably sought acceptance and recognition from the Fair Play for Cuba Committee. Oswald had few, if any, positive accomplishments he could point to in his life.
5. Oswald went to Mexico City in hopes of securing permission to travel to Cuba. It can only be assumed that he now viewed Cuba as the best place to be, just as he had once viewed the Soviet Union.
6. Oswald probably saw the assassination as a way to achieve the kind of special status his life lacked. The idea of killing JFK probably held immediate appeal for Oswald from the instant he first considered it.
7. Nosenko's knowledge of Oswald during his stay in Russia would have been useful to the CIA.

Kennedy in Dallas
Questions to Consider—page 16
1. Texas carries a large number of electoral votes, making it one of several key states in deciding the presidential election.
2. Presidents have to deal with many people from different regions, who will often have differing agendas. Not often will people of such diverse backgrounds think exactly alike on issues.
3. Although Austin is the capital of Texas, Kennedy probably chose to spend time in Dallas due to both its size and the convenience it afforded in meeting with people they needed to see on this trip. Kennedy had also planned to stay for a couple of days at the vice president's LBJ Ranch, nearer the Austin area.

The Assassination
Questions to Consider—page 21
1. Answers will vary. Kennedy was allowed to ride in an open convertible at a slow rate of speed. Agents were not stationed closely by him. Buildings along the motorcade route had open windows, etc. . . .
2. Answers will vary. Johnson was probably not rushing the transfer of power. A function of government this important, also outlined in the Constitution, cannot be delayed simply for sentimental reasons.

Apprehended!
Questions to Consider—page 23
1. Answers will vary. Oswald left his workplace immediately after the assassination without permission of his supervisors. Almost everything he did after that time indicates that he was fleeing.
2. Answers will vary, but Oswald's behavior indicates that he did not plan much beyond the assassination itself. Apparently, he had no plan in place for escape. By the time he was caught at the Texas Theater, federal agents were already aware that Oswald was missing from his workplace and were collecting evidence at the site of the School Book Depository.

Ruby
Questions to Consider—page 25
Answers will vary for this section.

The Funeral
Questions to Consider—page 28
1. Answers will vary, but Kennedy's personality seemed to embody some of the hopes and aspirations of the entire world.
2. Americans were both devastated and outraged that such a tragedy could happen in America during such good times. The controversy surrounding America's involvement in the war in Vietnam led thousands of Americans toward a peace movement that found millions of followers and spawned protest movements all over the United States. The Woodstock Music Festival in 1969 marked the peak of the peace movement. Flower power, drugs, rebellion, and protest were all a part of the changing face of America brought on initially by the assassination and funeral of President Kennedy.

Theories and Discrepancies
Questions to Consider—page 31
Due to the speculative nature of this particular section, answers will vary greatly.